From Ice Age to Essex

A history of the people and landscape of East London

Pamela Greenwood, Dominic Perring and Peter Rowsome

Published in 2006 by the
Museum of London Archaeology Service
part of the Museum of London Group

A CIP catalogue record for this book is available from the British Library

ISBN 1-901992-61-6

Front cover: view across a landscape of fields and woodland in the northern
part of the East London Gravels study area, looking north towards Cranham
Marsh from the Ockendon Road (photograph: Andy Chopping)
Back cover: a paleolithic handaxe from Ayletts Farm, Rainham; buttons from
World War I uniforms found buried at Hunts Hill Farm

Acknowledgements

This book has been made possible through the generous financial
sponsorship of the East London Gravels project by the Aggregates Levy
Sustainability Fund (ALSF), administered by English Heritage and supported by
the aggregates industry as part of their role in conservation and environmental
stewardship.

Support for the excavation work on the East London gravel sites came
from many sources. Funding and help in kind came from English Heritage,
the former Greater London Council, Essex County Council, and the London
Boroughs of Newham and Havering. Private developers and aggregates
companies also supported the work: London & Edinburgh Trust at Uphall
Camp; Redlands Aggregates at Hunts Hill Farm and other sites; Hoveringham's
at Great Arnold's Field; Cawoods at Moor Hall Farm; St Alban's Sand and Gravel
(later RMC) at Great Sunnings Farm; Ayletts (now Bretts) at Manor Farm; and
Redlands Aggregates (now Lafarge Aggregates) at Fairlop Quarry. Farmers and
tenants at the properties also gave essential support to the archaeological
investigations, along with the many volunteers who worked on the sites.

The authors would like to thank all the contributors to the recent
archaeological assessment of the East London gravels sites, carried out by
a team from MoLAS, Essex County Council Field Archaeology Unit (ECCFAU)
and the University of York. Particular thanks go to Julian Hill, Dan Swift and
Alison Telfer, of MoLAS, for their work on the site assessments and general
comments on this text, and to Patrick Allen of ECCFAU for his comments on
the Fairlop Quarry site. Thanks also go to Richard Bradley, of the University
of Reading, and Jane Corcoran, Nick Elsden, John Giorgi, Nick Holder and
Kevin Rielly, of MoLAS, for their contributions to the thematic chapter. Former
staff of the Passmore Edwards Museum and Newham Museum Archaeology
Service, who worked on the excavations, also provided help and advice.
We would also like to thank staff from English Heritage, particularly Brian
Kerr, Chris Scull and Barney Sloane; Nick Truckle at the Greater London
Archaeological Advisory Service; local authority planning departments and
local libraries, archives and museums for their support.

Special thanks must go to Nigel Brown of Essex County Council for his
kind advice and permission to use information and images from Finest
prospect: the archaeology of south Essex, published in 2005 and funded by
the ALSF. Other projects mentioned in this book include the ALSF-funded
Lea Valley project, undertaken by MoLAS in partnership with the British
Geological Survey, and West London landscapes, an English Heritage-funded
MoLAS publication of findings at Heathrow Airport.

All uncredited photographs are by Pam Greenwood. Other institutions
and individuals are thanked for their permission to reproduce illustrations.
Design, reprographics and production are by MoLAS, with artwork produced
by Sophie Lamb and special thanks to Sandra Rowntree and Faith Vardy for
picture research. The text was edited by Sue Hirst; project management was
by Peter Rowsome.

Contents

Foreword

This book presents a short history of human habitation in East London, based on archaeological findings at excavations on gravel extraction sites in the area. These include a group of sites investigated between 1963 and 1999 which are being analysed as part of the East London gravels project.

To find the beginning of this story and the true source of funding for this book, we have to go back half a million years to the advancing ice sheets that pushed the Thames southwards to its present course, depositing the series of terraces of river gravels that exist across East London today. These gravels have a huge commercial value and quarrying has evolved from ancient diggings to the modern aggregates industry.

Archaeological work on the East London gravels began when finds from gravel pits were given to local collectors and museums. Many spectacular discoveries belong to the era when gravel was dug by hand, such as a Roman stone coffin found near Dagenham in 1928 and the rich Early Saxon cemetery with glass drinking horns from Gerpin's Pit, Rainham, uncovered in 1937.

The main archaeological sites which make up this story are spread over a wide area of East London. Their names speak of a time before London's urban sprawl reached eastwards: Manor Farm, Great Sunnings Farm, Hunts Hill

Computer-generated view of the south edge of the Essex ice sheet

Farm, Whitehall Wood, Moor Hall Farm, Great Arnold's Field, Uphall Camp, Warren Farm and Fairlop Quarry. Most of these sites – excavated under what were sometimes harsh conditions – yielded important findings that have never before been published.

Map showing simplified drift geology and hydrology along the Lower Thames and the location of the East London gravels study area

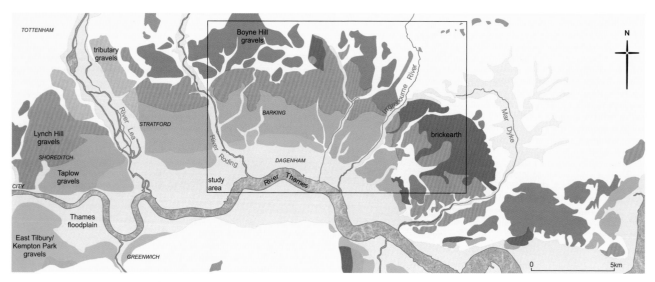

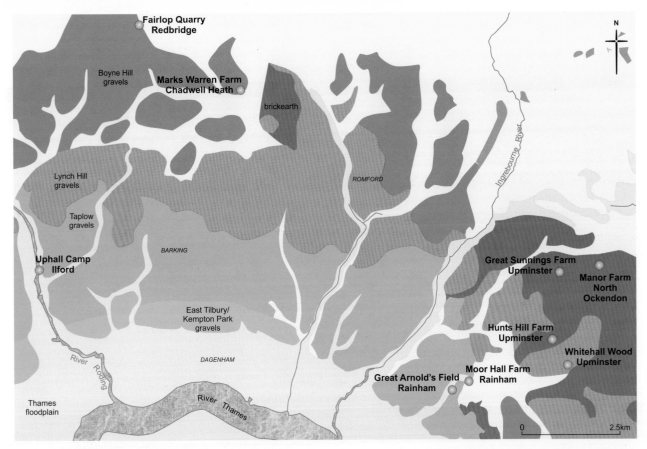

Map of the study area showing the nine East London gravels project archaeological sites (green dots) in relation to drift geology

Discoveries have revealed the ancient landscapes of East London and a history of human occupation from the 3rd millennium BC right up to the 19th century and later. The finds include evidence of where people lived, and how they made a living and viewed themselves. These settlement patterns, economic systems and cultural identities changed over time and contributed to the form of today's East London.

Abandoned gravel workings at Belhus Woods prior to restoration; the usable gravel has been taken away for processing and the poor quality material cast back in heaps

A post-war advertisement for Upminster sand and gravel

1

A history of the landscape and its people

Beginnings: the ages of ice and the first humans

The Palaeolithic (450,000–8000 BC)

London's landscape was forged by the River Thames. This riverside environment still remains obvious amidst the flatlands and marshes of the lower estuary. In other places bluffs and small islands established points of high ground from which the river's rich resources could best be exploited. These places drew early settlers and established the crossing points – fords, ferries and bridges – that moulded the human landscape of southern Britain. London owes its location and eminence to such factors.

The river only settled on its present course about 450,000 years ago, when climate change led to the Anglian glaciation, a huge ice sheet spreading south across the Thames valley as far as present-day Hornchurch, and forcing the river southwards. Before this time it took a more northerly route, heading east towards Clacton and the sea.

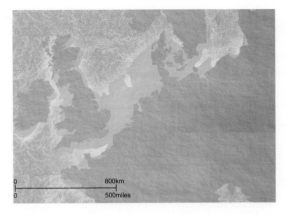

Sea levels were much lower at various stages in the past; this map shows the extent of land 12,000 years ago when Britain was connected to mainland Europe

Schematic section showing the gravel terraces and early courses of the River Thames in Essex

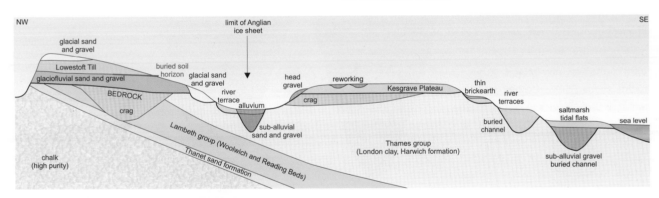

LEFT View of gravel extraction sites at Belhus Woods Country Park, near Aveley, where the Whitehall Wood and Hunts Hill Farm quarries have been restored to grassland, fishing lakes and fields

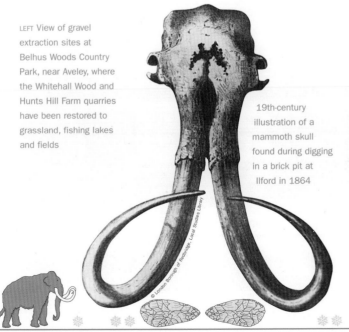

19th-century illustration of a mammoth skull found during digging in a brick pit at Ilford in 1864

The gravel terraces of East London and South Essex were created by the energetic waters of this earlier river. Ice ages came and went, and the climate alternated between arctic cold and more temperate warm periods. When ice was on the march, in the depths of the colder periods, glaciers pushed south to the borders of London, but in the balmier interludes deer and rhinoceros grazed here on open grassland. The very weight of the glaciers caused the land to buckle and heave. Such fluctuations have lifted the ground level, whilst melting glaciers have in turn fed rising sea levels. Because of these different stages of lifting and cutting, the oldest riverbeds now form the highest steps of the gravel terraces. These usually survive furthest from the present course of the river and were cut into by later river channels, into which younger beds of gravel were then deposited.

These different gravel terraces help us to describe different periods in the history of the river. They were deposited at a time when people first made their appearance in Britain. For most of this time Britain was not yet an island. The first hominids arrived here in the warmer periods, as they followed game north. These earliest visitors to Britain were not Homo sapiens, but they made and used flint tools, and operated as complex social groups. Sometimes their handaxes and other flint implements are found with the river gravels.

Comparatively little Palaeolithic material is known from London. At Woodford, however, roadworks for the M11 revealed four handaxes, a handaxe tip and nine flint flakes, recovered from near the surface of a gravel deposit. Palaeolithic axes have also been found at Moor Hall Farm but in layers that are later, suggesting that these objects may have been collected and treasured by ancient peoples.

But beyond these glimpses of passing hominid hunters this was a landscape without people. For much of the Ice Age the London region remained inhospitable arctic tundra. Human influence had yet to be felt in these wild and empty places.

Homo heidelbergensis hunters killing an elephant over 400,000 years ago in what is now southern Britain

Palaeolithic handaxe from Ayletts Farm, Rainham

In 1964 the remains of a woolly mammoth and straight tusked elephant were found in a gravel quarry at Sandy Lane, Aveley, near Moor Hall Farm

One of the Palaeolithic handaxes found at South Woodford during roadworks for the M11

450,000 BC

People on the move

The Mesolithic and Early Neolithic (8000–3500 BC)

Modern humans, *Homo sapiens*, arrived in north-west
Europe some 40,000 years ago in a phase of colonisation
that broadly coincided with the extinction of Neanderthal
man. But few such people ventured north to Britain and
permanent settlement did not take place until after the
retreat of the last main ice age around 11,000 BC. In East
London the first evidence for human activity dates to the early
Mesolithic (Middle Stone Age) period, in about 8000 BC.

Mesolithic sites are characterised by flint implements,
including microliths (small flints sometimes used to form
composite tools) and core axes, as well as other stone,
bone and antler artefacts. Early Mesolithic implements
were found at several of the East London gravels sites,
along the A13 and in Stratford. These tools attest to the
sporadic presence of hunter-gatherers who operated in the
wooded landscape that had replaced the open tundra as
the climate warmed. This environment can be reconstructed
from plant pollen preserved in the buried peat and clay.
Pollen from Enfield Lock in the Lea Valley illustrated the
spread of a pine forest replaced by mixed hazel and elm
woodland. Oak and then lime trees dominated the
woodland in the later Mesolithic, and was home to wild
cattle (aurochs), roe, red deer and boar. The hunters soon
found themselves island dwellers, as rising sea levels cut
Britain off from Continental Europe.

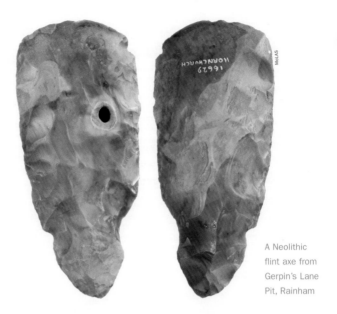

A Neolithic
flint axe from
Gerpin's Lane
Pit, Rainham

Much of the land familiar to these early hunters was
eventually settled for farming. Late Mesolithic flint tools
and Early Neolithic (New Stone Age) tools and pottery have
been found together at Brookway in Rainham. At Great
Arnold's Field a ritual monument or henge was represented
by a ring ditch about 15m in diameter. The ditch contained
Early Neolithic pottery
that included fine
burnished bowls.

Colonists from
Continental Europe
may have introduced
new ways of living –
the first cereals and
domestic animals all
had to be imported into
Britain. Farmers still
relied on flint tools, but
pottery was now also used.
It seems that the London
area was slow to adopt these
new practices and the earliest
farming in East London dates
to the middle of the 4th
millennium BC. Grain has been found at Beckton and
charred remains of emmer wheat in the Blackwater estuary.

Neolithic pottery from Great
Arnold's Field – a splendid
piece of Mildenhall ware

Examples of Mesolithic
flint artefacts; these are
from Hampstead Heath
in north London

Turning landscapes into places

The Late Neolithic and Early Bronze Age (3500 BC–1500 BC)

The scattered farming communities established in East London between 3500 and 3000 BC were probably engaged in pastoralism, with agricultural activity supplemented by hunting and gathering. The landscape was a mosaic of clearings against a backdrop of woodland.

Farming and settlement contributed to increasingly complicated social structures. Surplus labour was used to build monuments of earth and timber, generally on higher ground away from the river, as people established ties to the land that they occupied. The most impressive of these is a causewayed enclosure at Orsett, surrounded by substantial ditches with many entrances or causeways. Another may be represented by a substantial causewayed ditch recently recorded in advance of gravel extraction at Southall Farm, Rainham.

Sea levels rose, drowning the floodplain, and submerged woods have been found from Purfleet through Rainham to Dagenham and East Ham. A wooden trackway found at Silvertown was built in response to these changing conditions.

Artist's impression of Bronze Age hunters killing a wild cow or aurochs flushed from the forest

Reconstruction view of the Orsett Neolithic causewayed enclosure in c 3000 BC, with people arriving to take part in a ceremony

A Bronze Age perforated clay slab from Mucking; the function of these odd objects remains unknown

8000 BC   3500 BC

By 2500 BC – about the same time that Stonehenge was erected – 'Beaker culture', with a new-found knowledge of metalworking, was thriving in parts of what is now Germany. Beaker pottery – large drinking vessels thought to have been used in feasting – was introduced to Britain, suggesting that Beaker people had migrated from mainland Europe. Burial rites also changed, with graves now containing Beaker pots and other grave goods. These burials and their high-status contents may be evidence for the emergence of a hierarchical society. Powerful individuals dominated the agricultural communities and, through monuments like Stonehenge, charted the seasons that determined the success of their crops.

The Beaker pot from the Mucking burial

Overhead view of a Beaker burial found at Mucking

Evidence of 'Beaker culture' has come from several East London sites. At Great Arnold's Field, Beaker pots had been buried in a central pit surrounded by the earlier Neolithic ring ditch. Traces of Beaker settlement have also been found at Moor Hall Farm, Rainham Football Ground and Gerpin's Pit, Rainham. For some reason this 'Beaker culture' seems to have made little impact to the west of London.

An archaeologist excavating a Bronze Age cooking pit at the Royal Docks Community School in Newham; meat was roasted in the red-hot flints which filled the pit

Some of the flint arrowheads from the Beaker burial at Mucking

1500 BC · 750 BC · AD 50 · AD 200 · AD 400 · AD 1000 · AD 1500 · AD 2006

A landscape of farms and fields

Middle to Late Bronze Age (1500 BC–750 BC)

As the Bronze Age progressed, social and economic organisation grew. Those who occupied positions of power used fine bronze goods and weapons to display wealth and status. Burial was important to the presentation of power and many of Britain's barrows were built at this time. At Fairlop Quarry two ring ditches formed part of a ceremonial landscape associated with human burial – represented by pyre debris and cremations, some within 'Deverel-Rimbury' ceramic urns.

A Bronze Age trackway being excavated at Beckton

A pair of complete Middle Bronze Age Deverel-Rimbury pots – a bucket urn (left) and bowl

The pastoral landscape became more agricultural as more complex field systems and enclosures were set out. Sea and river levels continued to rise and trackways were built to link settlements on the dry gravel terraces, with riverside marshes and meadows used for the grazing of sheep or cattle.

One of the largest concentrations of Bronze Age metalwork in England has been recovered from the tidal Thames from Kingston to Woolwich, the River Lea and Barking Creek. Hoards of broken objects included knives, axes, adzes, hammers, swords, spears, harness fittings and occasionally jewellery. Prestigious artefacts were also thrown into rivers in 'votive' ritual, perhaps in fulfilment of a promise made to a deity. This disposable wealth may reflect increasing agricultural surpluses as farming intensified or the strength of the beliefs that people held.

A hoard of Bronze Age implements from Hacton, near Hornchurch, including socketed axe heads (top) and part of a spearhead (bottom right)

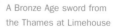

A Bronze Age sword from the Thames at Limehouse

More woodland was cleared for settlement after 1000 BC. Small communities established mixed farming on the gravel terraces, with fields, droveways and waterholes. Farm settlements were often out in the open but farmsteads were sometimes set inside bank-and-ditch enclosures, entered through a timber gate. Round houses stood within the enclosures. At South Hornchurch a central round house had a large porch facing the enclosure entrance. Other settlements were found at Uphall Camp and Hunts Hill Farm. People now had a wider variety of cooking and storage pots, together with fine jars, bowls and cups, perhaps reflecting new social attitudes to eating and drinking.

Late Bronze Age bowls from Mucking

View of the Late Bronze Age landscape and enclosures in the valley of the Ingrebourne, South Hornchurch

Iron Age (750 BC–AD 50)

The Iron Age was a time of hillforts – centres of political control amidst a warring tribal society. This was also a time of major social, economic and technological change. The introduction of ironworking was one sign of this and many of the circular enclosures of the Late Bronze Age landscape were abandoned. Some archaeologists believe that the layout of houses and streets within hillforts suggests a communal lifestyle with few distinctions in social status, though others feel they were only occupied during times of threat.

East London lies on the fringe of the hillfort zone to the west and the villages of Essex to the east. The landscape east of London was dominated by a major fortified settlement at Uphall Camp. Uphall lay beside the River Roding where it flowed into the Thames at Ilford, a strategic point which commanded the river terraces of East London and South Essex. A bank and ditch enclosed an area of 24 hectares, making Uphall one of the largest fortified sites known from England. Excavations have revealed round houses, rectangular structures and livestock enclosures. The discovery of three 'potin' coins – the earliest type of coinage used in Britain – are a sure sign of the site's importance. Uphall was abandoned by the early 1st century BC, a period when many other hillforts came and went.

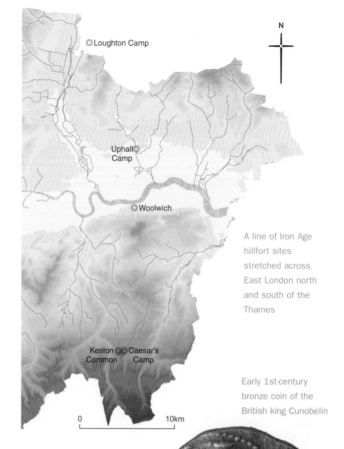

A line of Iron Age hillfort sites stretched across East London north and south of the Thames

Early 1st-century bronze coin of the British king Cunobelin

The Iron Age fortified town at Colchester

Uphall, with its low-lying site and its similarity to an oppidum (fortified town), differs from the typical hillfort, of which there were relatively few in the area. Nevertheless, the large hillfort sites at Loughton Camp, Uphall, Woolwich, Caesar's Camp and Keston appear to form a 'line'.

There were also other types of settlement. These included small, unenclosed farmsteads at Moor Hall Farm, enclosed and open settlements at Hunts Hill Farm and Fairlop Quarry, and sprawling open villages such as Mucking. The absence of imported pottery indicates that such settlements were not part of long-distance trade networks.

After 150 BC, agricultural growth demanded new fields and settlements. The population grew, even though it was a time of climate deterioration, and more marginal land was cultivated, although some fields were abandoned because of soil exhaustion.

After Caesar's expeditions to Britain in 55–54 BC, south-east Britain came under the growing influence of Rome and Gaul. Coinage reflects the formation of kingdoms with close ties to Rome. According to Caesar, some parts of the south-east were settled by immigrants from Gaul. East London fell within the control of a territory of the Trinovantes that was ruled by Cunobelin – Shakespeare's Cymbeline – whose capital was established at Colchester. Imported amphorae (storage vessels) show that Roman consumption patterns were being adopted by British society.

A series of single-, double- and triple-ditched enclosures

A Roman amphora, used for importing wine from the Continent, found in a Late Iron Age water hole at Hunts Hill Farm; reconstructed complete amphora profile to right

are characteristic of the Late Iron Age in this part of Britain. Triple-ditched enclosures have been found at Moor Hall Farm and Orsett Cock. A well within the Moor Hall Farm enclosure included a large 'termination' deposit – a ritual offering – of Late Iron Age pottery.

The Late Iron Age triple-ditched enclosure at Orsett

1st-century AD pots found in a Late Iron Age well at Moor Hall Farm

© Essex County Council

A distant power: annexation by Rome

Early Roman (AD 50–200)

Britain was annexed by Rome after the invasion of AD 43, in a campaign of conquest initiated by the Emperor Claudius. This historical event had a profound impact. Colchester was captured and became the site of a veteran colony, whilst a new city called Londinium was founded at the present-day City of London. These new towns were important centres for the imperial administration. Their construction involved the introduction of a range of new architectural and social ideas.

Roads aligned on the bridge at London became major features in the landscape and attracted roadside villages, such as Old Ford on the road from London to Colchester.

Roman coin of the Emperor Claudius

Map of the Roman road network in south-east England

Despite this, the countryside changed remarkably little in the opening years of Roman rule. New farmsteads, crops and techniques had arrived in the late pre-Roman Iron Age. Ceramic assemblages also show patterns of continuity from the Late Iron Age, as storage jars remain more common than the new tablewares.

It is often assumed that Londinium must have promoted trade by taking rural produce and supplying goods to rural communities in return, but there is little evidence that this happened on any significant scale in the East London area. Some new foodstuffs did arrive – the backfill of disused Roman wells at Hunts Hill Farm included carrot, coriander and celery seeds, perhaps from a local kitchen garden, and the head of a honey bee, one of only six known in Roman Britain.

View of Roman London in the early 2nd century; its location on the tidal Thames was a suitable point to bridge the river and develop a port

The Roman farmstead and villa at Mucking

At Moor Hall Farm Roman field systems replaced the triple-ditched enclosure. Where houses have been found, as at Fairlop Quarry, they appear to have been built in a pre-Roman style – the round houses dated to the late 1st or early 2nd century AD. Burial practices did change, with Roman cremation cemeteries found at Uphall Camp, Hunts Hill Farm, Manor Farm and Fairlop Quarry.

Very few villas were imposed on the Iron Age settlement landscape, and most of these were located in Kent. It is impossible to know whether the farms on the river terraces were owned by locals who saw no need to adopt Romano-British ways, or whether absentee landlords used rents and tithes to live in Roman style elsewhere.

Samian cup found in a burial at Hunts Hill Farm; a stamp on the base of the cup reads Siicundinus

Roman roof tiles (tegulae) which were laid together in the bottom of a well at Hunts Hill Farm

Getting more from the land: Late Antiquity

Late Roman (AD 200–400)

One of the more fascinating aspects of the archaeological study of landscapes is how they challenge our expectations. Whilst the Roman conquest appears to have had comparatively little impact on the lives of the people farming on the gravel terraces of East London, major changes did take place a century later. This was supposedly one of the 'golden' periods of Roman rule: a time of peace and prosperity.

At a period when one might expect demand to have been at a peak, there was a decline in the number of rural settlements, although the area being farmed did not shrink, and field systems were built at sites such as Fairlop Quarry in the 2nd–4th centuries. This late Roman landscape may have been more concerned with arable farming and with cattle, although sheep farming remained important. Late Roman boundary ditches at Fairlop Quarry may have formed a droveway, and fragments of lava quern suggest that crop processing was also taking place there.

Small late Roman bowl from London in Oxfordshire red colour-coated ware; late Roman pots in this ware were found at Hunts Hill Farm

Artist's reconstruction view of Roman Colchester in *c* AD 250

Artist's reconstruction of a late Roman burial ceremony

The 1928 discovery of a Roman coffin at South Hornchurch

It seems likely that these changes reflect the creation of larger estates and that investment in farm and stock improvement was intended to increase surplus production. But by the end of the 2nd century Londinium was contracting. It seems more likely that the larger crops were needed to meet the increasing demands of externally imposed taxes, rents and tithes. Imperial profitability could no longer depend on the spoils of conquest, so attention had turned to making more from the territories that had already been conquered.

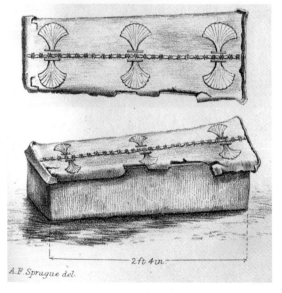

A.F. Sprague del.

Ornate late Roman lead coffins found, along with a stone coffin and about 20 cremation urns, during gravel digging near East Ham church in 1863

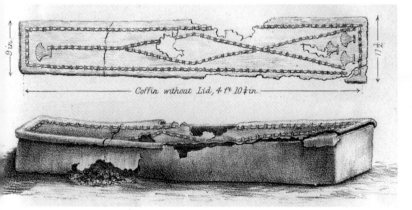

Coffin without Lid, 4 ft 10⅞ in.

AD 1000   AD 1500   AD 2006

From the East Saxons to Essex

Early medieval (AD 400–1000)

The Roman administration of Britain collapsed in the early 5th century due to political, economic and military pressure. The events of the subsequent 'dark ages' are hard to identify or date. Britain was no longer regularly supplied with Roman coin, whilst the more distinctive types of datable tablewares were no longer in fashion. Historical records are also rare, since the 5th- and 6th-century Anglo-Saxons or locals were non-literate. Later chronicles describe the settlement of Germanic peoples and state that most of eastern England was under Anglo-Saxon rule by the end of the 5th century. By the late 6th century the London region was a province of an East Saxon kingdom.

Glass bead and pot from Early Saxon burials at Hunts Hill Farm

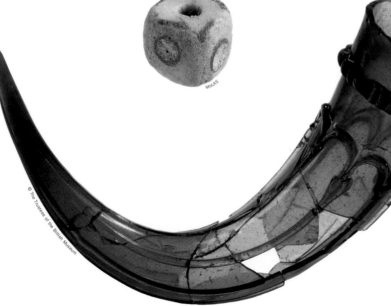

Artist's view of the Mucking Early Saxon settlement on a winter's day

Early Saxon settlements in East London were undefended villages and farmsteads concentrated along the Thames and its tributaries. Only a few of these rural settlements have been excavated. The basis of the Saxon economy was agricultural, but few examples of their field systems have been found. Farming was probably less intense than in the Roman period, with some forest regeneration on the borders of farmland and a return to pasture.

A beautiful and rare glass drinking horn from Gerpins Pit, Rainham

AD 50

AD 200

AD 400

Many early Saxon settlements were established on land that had been farmed in Roman times and 5th-century cemeteries were sometimes located near Roman settlements. A few graves, bereft of human remains, were recorded alongside a late Roman ditch at Hunts Hill Farm. A splendid group of 6th-century pagan Saxon burials was also found during gravel digging at Gerpins Pit, Rainham, in the 1930s; it contained two fine glass drinking horns as well as spears and shield bosses.

Gravel quarrying at Mucking in the 1970s with an Early Saxon sunken-floored building visible in the foreground

The 7th-century Prittlewell burial chamber discovered at Southend: an East Saxon king?

Grave goods from Early Saxon burials at Mucking, including brooches, beads and a glass spindle whorl

Although Londinium had apparently been abandoned at the end of the Roman period, a new urban settlement of *Lundenwic* developed slightly upstream during the 7th century. After Viking attacks in the 9th century, King Alfred re-established the town within the protection of the old Roman defences. The late Saxon period saw the English landscape of towns, villages and farms take form.

London as capital city

From the Norman Conquest to the Reformation (AD 1000–1500)

Rural settlement continued to shift and change during the early medieval period, resulting in the formation of villages such as Rainham, Wennington and Aveley. London became the capital of England and the surrounding countryside witnessed considerable growth, although a sharp decline followed in the 14th century, partly a consequence of the Black Death.

Most of the late medieval villages remained occupied until they were swallowed up by the growing metropolis. The late medieval landscape of London's hinterland is poorly understood archaeologically, as many of these villages are hidden beneath modern town centres, but there seems to have been more settlement in the north and west of London. An improvement in climate meant that the countryside around London saw large increases in agricultural production, domestic livestock and woodland management. Later medieval settlements have been found in West Ham, Barking and Dagenham.

Part of an enclosed Saxo-Norman farmstead recorded at Great Arnold's Field was associated with important 12th-century pottery, suggesting that the site had connections beyond the local area. A 12th-century timber 'hall-house' was excavated at Hunts Hill Farm and other finds suggest that an earlier medieval settlement lay nearby. The Domesday Book mentions a manor, thought to be situated on Hunts Hill Farm, occupied by someone called Mauger.

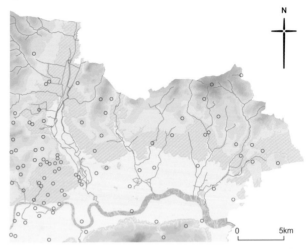

Map showing the location of the many known medieval villages in East London

The medieval pottery was very different from that found in central London, suggesting that the East London sites lay in a peripheral area, with most trade moved along the coast rather than inland.

Excavation of a timber-framed medieval hall house at Hunts Hill Farm

AD 50

AD 200

AD 400

The growth of London

From 1500 to the present

The post-medieval history of the Lower Thames estuary is dominated by the growth of London, whose economic and environmental impacts have profoundly altered the landscape.

In 1550 London was already a large city with a population of 120,000. London's appetite for grain and fuel, which included straw, wood, charcoal and coal, continued to grow. Several manors around London specialised in fuel supply but imported coal was becoming increasingly important, allowing woodland to be cleared for grazing, tillage or horticulture. Coal use resulted in the great smogs for which London was once so famous. The grain supply came from a wide area and even in 1570 corn was being imported from the South Midlands. The demand for grain encouraged arable farming in areas with suitable soil and good transport. Sites closer to the city specialised in dairying and market gardens.

More than anything else London needed people. Despite high levels of urban mortality, the towns offered employment and greater social mobility, whilst the wealthy established their houses in places like West Ham, Leyton and Wanstead, until the expansion of industry made these areas less pleasant.

Broadfields Barn, built in the 17th century; one of the best preserved barns in the London area, it forms part of the Thames Chase Visitor Centre at Pike Lane, Cranham, Upminster

The march of brick – a Victorian cartoon emphasising the impact of London's growth on the surrounding countryside

Pigs being driven to market along a main street in 19th-century Romford

Haggling at the market stall;
Romford Market in about 1855

By 1801 London was home to over a million people.
The city continued to grow, with row upon row of new
Victorian houses built by an army of immigrant workmen.
Whitehall Wood was the site of a local brick kiln in use in
the 19th century and up to the 1920s, and now restored.
New housing east of Barking and Ilford came with the
19th-century expansion of the railways to Dagenham,
Romford and beyond, and the Underground from Barking
to Upminster in 1932.

Artist's view of the Battle of Britain; East London docks
and industries were primary targets and central to the
fight for air supremacy

Advertisements of
the 1930s for new
healthier housing
for London workers

AD 50 AD 200 AD 400

After World War I village life started to disappear and much of Dagenham was demolished to make way for a new estate. These huge new town estates replaced crowded and filthy East End slums, rehousing war veterans, and providing manual workers and their families with homes and gardens. Ford Motors added to employment opportunities from the 1920s, and shipbuilding and industry continued to expand along the Thames at Dagenham and Rainham.

Dagenham, Upminster and Rainham remained important market gardening areas until recent times. At Uphall Camp a 16th-century farm flourished until the 19th century. A 17th-century windmill stood on the Iron Age earthworks there, which were visible until the 1960s. The archaeology of East London also includes other oddities, such as World War II gun emplacements and military installations, reflecting the looming presence of Central London.

Aerial view of the Ford Motor Company Ltd plant at Dagenham in 1949–50

View of the London Cement loading jetty, upriver from Creekmouth at Dagenham Docks

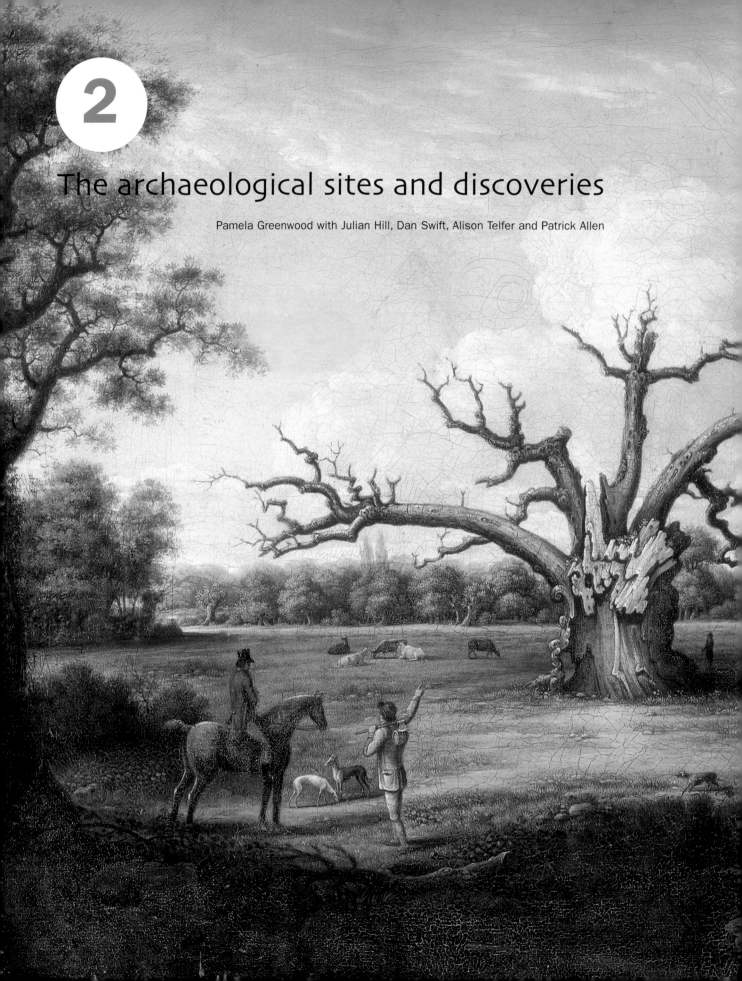

2

The archaeological sites and discoveries

Pamela Greenwood with Julian Hill, Dan Swift, Alison Telfer and Patrick Allen

Hunts Hill and Whitehall Wood, Upminster

Hunts Hill Farm and Whitehall Wood lie on the same gravel plateau about 20m above sea level, at the southern tip of Upminster parish. Dry summers in the late 1970s caused cropmarks to appear on farmland at Hunts Hill Farm, leading to the discovery of the archaeological sites. Both sites now form part of the Thames Chase Community Forest. Whitehall Wood is part of Belhus Woods ancient woodland and the quarry pit is now a deep lake. Hunts Hill Farm, a working quarry until recently, is not yet fully restored.

The first people at Hunts Hill Farm settled there during the Middle Bronze Age. Archaeologists have found slight traces of their settlement – just a few pits and postholes. A pottery jar buried in the ground with a piece of quartz inside may have been an offering to gods or spirits. Late Bronze Age people built timber round houses and fences, and dug ditches and wells. They continued the tradition of burying pots, and one special pit held at least 28 smashed pots. To the south, farmers laid out fields at Whitehall Wood.

Early Bronze Age barbed and tanged flint arrowhead from a posthole at Hunts Hill Farm

The main archaeological features at Whitehall Wood were field boundaries, reflecting many centuries of subsistence agriculture

Excavation of a Late Bronze Age pit containing smashed pots at Hunts Hill Farm

LEFT: Detail from 'The Fairlop Oak, Hainault Forest', 1816

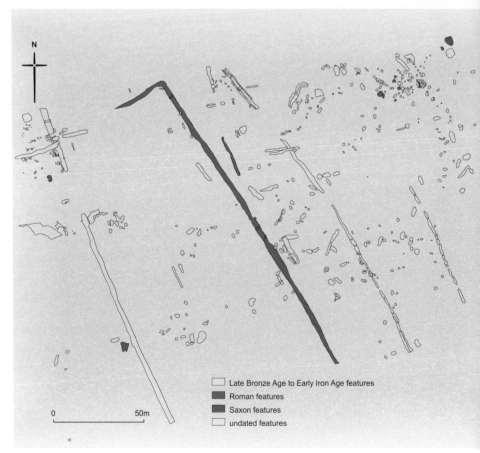

N

Late Bronze Age to Early Iron Age features
Roman features
Saxon features
undated features

0   50m

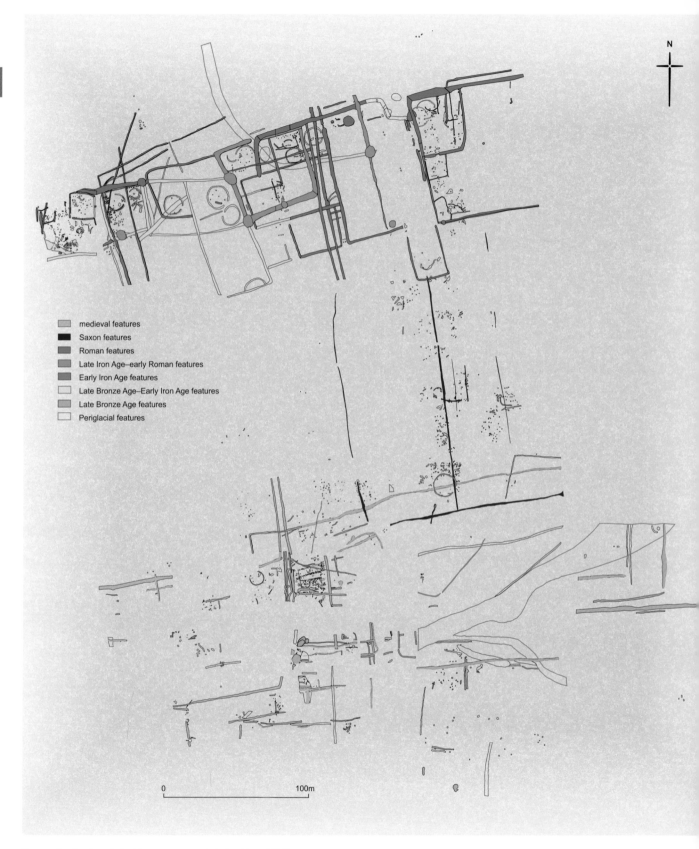

N

	medieval features
	Saxon features
	Roman features
	Late Iron Age–early Roman features
	Early Iron Age features
	Late Bronze Age–Early Iron Age features
	Late Bronze Age features
	Periglacial features

0   100m

Thousands of archaeological features were recorded at Hunts Hill Farm,
and included field boundaries, water holes, hut circles and buildings

Base of a flint-gritted Bronze Age jar from Hunts Hill Farm

In the Iron Age people still buried deliberately damaged pots in small pits and wells, sometimes with an attractive pebble – offerings to keep the wells sweet or a termination rite. They kept animals – there are several large wells and waterholes, and some of these contained dung beetles and bracken, which may have been used as fodder. At least ten round houses at Hunts Hill Farm date to this period, along with a small bronze smithy. At the end of the Iron Age a large rectangular enclosure, about 60m by 50m, with a gateway facing north, dominated the hill.

Late Bronze Age to Early Iron Age pots and pebbles from Hunts Hill Farm

An Iron Age round house at Hunts Hill Farm

Excavation of an Early Iron Age water hole at Hunts Hill Farm

After the Roman conquest much of Hunts Hill Farm was used as farmland, with more fields and animal paddocks laid out. A waterhole or well contained what may be a special offering of holly leaves (a sacred tree) and bramble twine. The wells were roughly made, unlike the professional carpentry found in Londinium. Roman pottery and glass at the north-west corner of the site may indicate where people lived.

A Late Iron Age or early Roman glass bead found in a ditch at Hunts Hill Farm

Late Roman folded beaker found in a pit at Hunts Hill Farm

Hunts Hill Farm has many boundaries and alignments that lasted for hundreds, if not thousands, of years. This continuity suggests that the same people and their descendants may have lived here. The Saxon settlement may have lain at the southern end of Hunts Hill Farm, where there was a well and traces of a timber house. Early Saxon people were also living at Whitehall Wood and to the south-east around Aveley.

Hunts Hill Farm became part of a medieval ridge and furrow field system which survived until 1989, when the topsoil was finally removed. During the 20th century the site was a garden centre, which also sold fodder and hay, gas canisters and Christmas trees. World War I uniforms were buried in the soil to act as fertilizer and hundreds of buttons have been dug up.

Buttons from World War I uniforms; the uniforms were buried as fertilizer at Hunts Hill Farm

Base of a Roman well framework of second-hand timbers, including elm, excavated at Hunts Hill Farm

Moor Hall Farm and Great Arnold's Field, Rainham

Moor Hall Farm and Great Arnold's Field are separated by Launders Lane as it winds down towards the old London Road, the A13. The sites lie close to the edge of the Thames marshes on a gravel spur about 6–8m above sea level, higher than much of Rainham parish. Moor Hall Farm was a dairy until 1974, when problems with cattle rustling forced a switch to cereals, potatoes and vegetables.

The earliest finds from Moor Hall Farm are fragments of Early Palaeolithic handaxes and Great Arnold's Field was the site of a Neolithic ritual monument – a large ring ditch or henge. About 2000 years later, people using Beaker pottery settled at Moor Hall Farm and reused the sacred site at Great Arnold's Field. Late Bronze Age people dug pits and settled on the crest of the hill at Moor Hall Farm. About 500 years later this same spot was the site of a small Middle Iron Age village or large farm. A nearby well contained a pointed wooden stake, perhaps an offering to the gods.

At some point during the Middle Iron Age people started constructing the triple-ditched enclosure that came to dominate the higher ground at Moor Hall Farm, with a commanding view towards the Wennington and Thames marshes.

Excavating postholes and ditches associated with a Middle Iron Age round house at Moor Hall Farm

The reconstructed Middle Iron Age settlement at Butser Ancient Farm in Hampshire; many of the small settlements in East London may have looked something like this

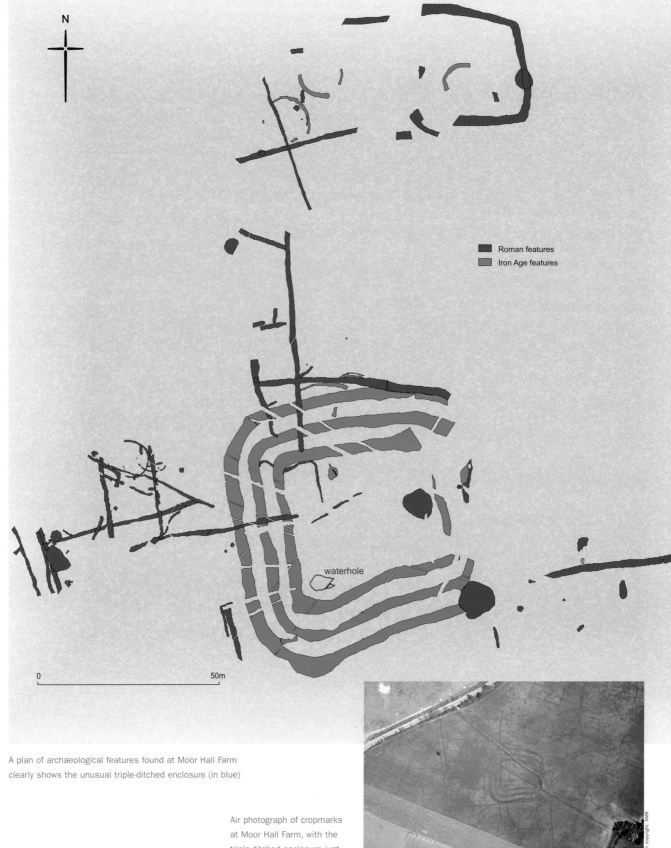

N

Roman features
Iron Age features

waterhole

0   50m

A plan of archaeological features found at Moor Hall Farm
clearly shows the unusual triple-ditched enclosure (in blue)

Air photograph of cropmarks
at Moor Hall Farm, with the
triple-ditched enclosure just
visible in the centre

© Crown copyright. NMR

A fine group of early
1st-century AD pots from
a Late Iron Age well at Moor Hall Farm; currently
on display in the 'London before London' gallery
at the Museum of London

By the end of the Late Iron Age the enclosure was complete, measuring about 80m across and with an east-facing entrance. It appears to have been a sacred enclosure, with people living just to the east of it. There were traces of 'ramparts' between some of the ditches but not internally. The claustrophobic, closely packed ditches and banks left a small central space just 25m across, occupied by a gully packed with fired clay and iron objects, a well and little else. The well had been back-filled with over 1000 freshly broken pots and a few other objects, and may represent a termination rite – perhaps a final farewell party – at the time of the Roman conquest.

The base of a late Roman timber-lined well discovered at Moor Hall Farm

A late Roman flint-lined well at Moor Hall Farm

During the Roman period the area was divided into fields, and cropmarks show that some of these extended into Great Arnold's Field. Towards the end of the Roman period a farmyard or settlement was established on the ancient route of Launders Lane.

Several centuries later the area is mentioned in the Domesday Survey as Launders Manor. The manor house may have stood near Launders barn on the eastern edge of the Moor Hall Farm site; alternatively a 12th-century farmstead, seen on aerial photographs and excavated at Great Arnold's Field in 1963, may be the site of the missing manor.

Great Sunnings Farm, Upminster, and Manor Farm, North Ockendon

Great Sunnings Farm and Manor Farm lie east of Upminster, in an area of higher gravel terrace still used for arable farming and market gardening, though also subject to intensive gravel extraction. Great Sunnings Farm was one of several 16th- and 17th-century farms around Corbets Tey.

Extensive cropmarks recorded at Great Sunnings Farm were found to be Late Iron Age enclosures and Roman field systems. No cropmarks were recorded in the excavated area at Manor Farm. Cropmarks have been seen in the fields between Great Sunnings Farm and Manor Farm, and Roman pottery was found here but little else is known about the archaeology.

At Manor Farm, a few stray Mesolithic flint implements were found. The next surviving evidence of people in the area is thousands of years later, when someone dug pits at Great Sunnings Farm in the Early Iron Age. Some of the pits contained burnt bone, and wheat and barley grains, possibly offerings to spirits.

View of heavy machinery engaged in topsoil stripping at Manor Farm

Field boundaries, ditches and other features at Great Sunnings, recreated from an excavator's sketch map

Aerial photograph of Great Sunnings cropmarks clearly shows the Late Iron Age enclosures and Roman field system; north at top

© Crown copyright. NMR

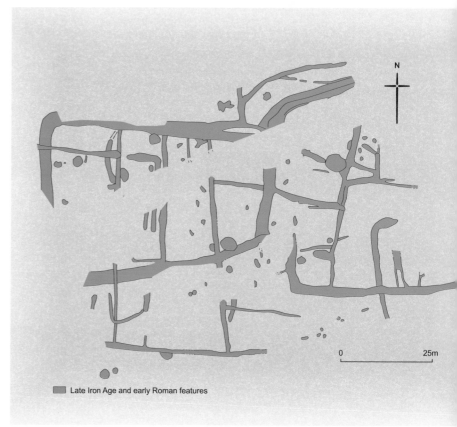

Late Iron Age and early Roman features

0   25m

During the later Iron Age a pair of large, roughly rectangular defensive enclosures dominated Great Sunnings Farm. These were linked and had steep-sided ditches. An Iron Age slingshot may have been used by defenders of the site, whose defences went out of use at the time of the Roman conquest. People still lived here during the early Roman period, establishing a system of long, narrow fields, dumping rubbish in the old ditches, and digging wells or waterholes for their stock.

An Iron Age slingshot projectile from Great Sunnings Farm

Excavating an early Roman cremation burial at Manor Farm

At Manor Farm a small, early Roman cemetery contained five cremation burials, including a young woman whose ashes were placed in a pottery flagon. Some were buried with pottery jars and small flagons, probably for special liquids. People used the site throughout the Roman period but they may have been poorer than their neighbours at Hunts Hill Farm and Moor Hall Farm.

At Great Sunnings Farm Late Iron Age rectangular defensive enclosures are just visible where archaeologists have begun excavating the ditches; quarrying work continues in the background

Smashed Roman pottery found in a ditch at Great Sunnings Farm

Quarrying work encroaching onto farmland at Manor Farm

The Great Sunnings farmhouse buildings on Sunnings or Sullens Lane, as they appeared decades ago

A few fragments of Early Saxon pottery show that people continued to live on the Manor Farm site. The farm lay in the Manor of (North) Ockendon, which was held by Earl Harold before 1066. Manor Farm includes boundaries which people established and maintained for thousands of years, with 20th-century hedgerows on the same alignment as prehistoric and Roman ditches.

Sunnings Lane forms part of the old 'Green Lane' that leads down past Hunts Hill Farm and Whitehall Wood towards Aveley. This line is one of several in a group of parallel parish boundaries, possibly old droveways leading to the marshland pastures.

A rural scene at one of the East London gravels sites belies the presence of London's surrounding urban sprawl

Marks Warren Farm, Chadwell Heath

Marks Warren Farm lies high above this part of the Thames Valley, commanding views from Hornchurch to the City. It is best known for the medieval moated manor of Marks, named after Simon de Merk, who bought it in 1330. The manor was carefully located to enjoy the advantages of the parish of Dagenham and especially the Liberty of Havering-atte-Bower. The house, Marks Hall, was demolished in 1805, but a boundary marker, the 'Warren Stone' survives. The medieval moat can still be identified, lying in thick undergrowth, and evidence of ridge and furrow fields survives nearby. The only other visible traces of the past are World War II anti-aircraft gun emplacements set back slightly from the crest of the hill and used to defend Hornchurch Aerodrome in the valley below.

Archaeological investigations in 1988 revealed a large prehistoric enclosure, Roman occupation and a medieval mill site, and as a result these were saved from gravel extraction, though not from plough damage.

View from Marks Warren Farm, Hornchurch, looking towards Brentwood

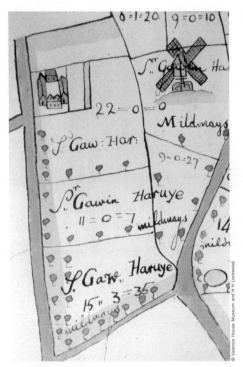

Copy of *c* 1618 map of Manor of Marks, showing Marks Manor House, its fields and a windmill

© Valence House Museum and H H Lockwood

© Crown copyright. NMR

The World War II anti-aircraft gun emplacements (encircled by tracks) on the hill at Marks Warren Farm

The 'Warren Stone', a boundary marker at Marks Warren Farm

The earliest traces of human activity are Mesolithic flint microliths and Neolithic or Early Bronze Age pottery and flint implements. During the Late Bronze Age a circular enclosure about 100m in diameter was constructed on the highest point of the gravel – 40m above sea level. It had deep, steep-sided ditches and a defended western entrance. People had dumped fine, decorated Early Iron Age pottery near the entrance when the ditches were almost silted up, perhaps to mark the end of its use.

A large triple-ditched enclosure built around the time of the Roman conquest can be identified from aerial photographs. The ditches were narrow and shallow, and may mark a boundary rather than a serious attempt to keep anything out. A narrow gravel track led to the enclosure and was flanked by a small building. Roman ditches were found on the hillside, and one contained samian ware depicting erotic scenes, which was precious enough to have been repaired with lead wire.

Investigating the early Roman triple-ditched enclosure at Marks Warren Farm; volunteers are beginning to excavate parts of each ditch

A fragment of samian ware found in a Roman ditch, showing an erotic scene

Late Bronze Age plain ware coarse jar from lowest fills of circular enclosure

There is ample evidence of medieval occupation, including a cottage. The Liberty was just over the border from the manor of Barking and free from Barking Abbey's restrictions, meaning that windmills were allowed. A number were set up, taking advantage of the windy site. In 1365 the manor was sold with a windmill called 'Le Newemille'.

Marks Warren Farm paddock; traces of ridge and furrow, the result of medieval ploughing, have been identified in the field in the background

The mill stood east of Marks Hall and is believed to have been demolished around 1760. The Marks Gate Mill, later Drakes Mill, is said to have been the largest in Essex and a brick tithe barn still stands on the site.

An inventory of 1479 describes the manor, listing crops of wheat, rye, oats and peas. The rest of the land was pasture and 14 cows were kept on a parcel of marsh five miles away. Stock included 12 cows, a bull, a calf, young bullocks, 20 goats (for milk and cheese), 17 ewes and lambs, a ram, 40 pigs and piglets, 3 carthorses, 2 plough oxen, 11 plough horses and some old stock inland, with some cattle on other farms. Hens, geese, ducks and peacocks remained at the farmyard. Today Marks Warren Farm is used for mixed arable farming, especially potatoes. This is the only manor in Dagenham still farmed today, by John Fowler and his family.

Late 18th-century view of the moated manor house at Marks, Dagenham

Fairlop Quarry, Redbridge

Fairlop lies north-west of Marks Warren Farm, overlooking the Thames Valley, and is said to be named for the 'Fair Lop Oak', an ancient tree which measured 30 feet in girth. An annual fair founded by Daniel Day (1682–1767) took place in the tree's shade on the first Friday of July, beginning sometime in the 1720s. By the 1750s the fair attracted large crowds and in 1765 the local constabulary reported that 'a great many people meet in a riotous and tumultous manner selling ale and spiritous liquors and keeping tippling booths and gaming tables to the great encouragement of vice and immorality'. Despite attempts to ban it, and the loss of the dying tree in a gale in 1820, the fair continued until 1856. According to local tradition, Day was buried in a coffin made from a branch lopped from the tree, but it was already called 'Fairlop' when Queen Anne 'to Hainault Forest did ride'. The tree was pollarded (ie lopped) but was so large and old that Chapman and André put it on their Essex map in 1772.

View of heavy machinery excavating gravel at Fairlop Quarry, with London in the distance

View of the fair beneath the Fairlop oak in 1817

© London Borough of Redbridge, Local Studies Library

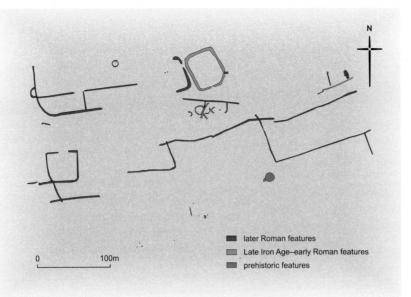

Plan of late Roman
field systems at
Fairlop Quarry

later Roman features
Late Iron Age–early Roman features
prehistoric features

0   100m

A reconstructed
Bronze Age palstave
(axe); a similar axe
head was found at
Fairlop

© Dominic Andrews, courtesy of the Portable Antiquities Scheme

The area was cleared for farmland in 1857 and parts
of it were later levelled for construction of a World War I
and II airfield. Fairlop was considered for the location of
London's airport after the war, but this was rejected and
gravel extraction became the dominant use.

Early occupation included two Middle Bronze Age ring
ditches, which marked out burial mounds containing
cremations and funeral pyres. An Iron Age settlement,
made up of round houses enclosed by defensive ditches,
was abandoned in the early Roman period and also
became a burial site.

The main Roman settlement was about 1km to the
north, where round houses and a second defended
enclosure gave way to large-scale agriculture in the later
Roman period. A sunken-floored building containing
fragments of quern and charred grain may have been
used for crop processing and is one of only a few
examples of Romano-British buildings from the
hinterland of Londinium. The site was completely
abandoned at the end of the Roman period and
reverted to forest until cleared in the 19th century
for farming.

© London Borough of Redbridge, Redbridge Museum

A flagon, probably containing
a votive offering, found in an
early Roman cremation pit at
Fairlop Quarry

Uphall Camp, Ilford

Many local people have heard of Uphall Camp, either as a supposed Danish Camp or as the site of a 20th-century chemical works. In fact it is far older than the Viking period. It was described by Lysons in 1796 and surveyed several times in the 19th century. From 1900 onwards the site almost disappeared under housing and a factory, although telltale bumps and boundaries hinted at the line of massive ditches and ramparts.

Howard's Chemical Works, built in 1899, produced aspirin, quinine, gas lamp mantles, luminous paint, solvents and denture powder during World War I. The factory grew and in 1960 the last surviving stretch of the ramparts, topped by what may have been a 17th- or 18th-century windmill mound, was destroyed.

Bark tips from the quinoa tree, used to make quinine at Howard's Chemical Works

The fort ditch and ramparts in 1926, with the chemical factory to the left

Hunters and fishermen first frequented the marshes along the River Roding in the Mesolithic and Neolithic periods, although there is no clear evidence that people lived here. In the 2nd century BC a massive fort was built on the gravel knoll. The fort guarded Barking Creek and may have faced a similar enclosure south of the Thames at Woolwich. With ditches several metres deep and ramparts at least 6m high, it would have been an impressive sight.

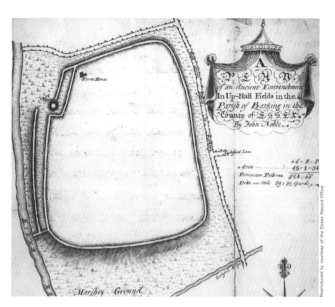

Noble's map of Uphall Camp showing a double set of earthworks on the River Roding, as described in the Lyson and Crouch survey

It seems likely that Uphall was an important tribal or political centre on the western boundary of the land of the Trinovantes tribe. An unfeasibly large number of people would have been needed to defend it, suggesting that its size was primarily intended to impress.

Two groups of round houses were built inside the area, with a clear zone in front of the ramparts forming a 'military way' or access area. Each group of houses included an enclosure, for animals or for marking out the main house, and nearby four-post buildings associated with burnt cereal grain and interpreted as raised granaries. Pots and other objects found in the drip gullies of the round houses may have been intentionally placed there. The main western entrance to the 'Camp' lay beside a little creek off the Roding, emphasising the inhabitants' connection with the river and trade. A shale bracelet from Dorset and the three potin coins point to long-distance contacts, although large pottery cauldrons speak of a local trading network as well.

A selection of Iron Age potin coins; similar examples were found at Uphall Camp

The important fortified Iron Age settlement at Uphall Camp

Sometime in the 1st century BC Uphall Camp was abandoned. Some activity can be dated to the early Roman period, when large quantities of Roman pottery were dumped into the disused ditches. Flagons and other pots normally used for feasting suggest that the abandoned earthwork was a sacred site. Finds included a coin of Severus Alexander and an iron knife still in its sheath.

Early Saxon inhabitants left few traces, but during the medieval period Uphall Camp became the site of the manor of Uphall, later Uphall Farm. Night soil brought from London to Barking Quay was dumped on the fields, and 19th-century orchards were used as a picnic spot.

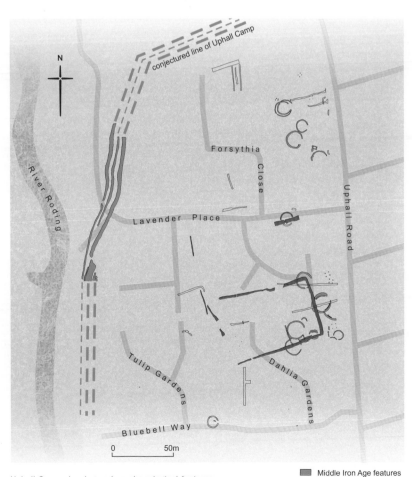

Uphall Camp showing main archaeological features, including ditches, enclosures and circular huts; related to modern street map

■ Middle Iron Age features
■ Roman features
☐ undated features

3

Themes and landscapes
The London region's landscapes compared and contrasted

The Lea Valley – a look into prehistory

Jane Corcoran

The River Lea joins the Thames to the west of the East London gravel sites. Its prehistoric levels lie deeply buried beneath later alluvium, which is in turn obscured by urban and industrial sprawl, but study of borehole data has allowed us to map the sub-surface of the ancient landscape.

Prehistoric occupation on the upland river terraces of the East London gravels was part of the exploitation of a wider landscape. The upland was dissected by many river valleys, now mostly hidden and forgotten, draining into the Thames. In the Lea Valley, archaeological work has revealed temporary Mesolithic camps, Bronze Age and Iron Age artefacts, Saxon boats and medieval water mills, reflecting the ways in which earlier inhabitants have used the resources of the valley for food, transport, industry and religious ritual.

The Lea and other river valleys acted as 'sinks', collecting environmental remains transported by wind, water, gravity and human activity. Prehistoric activity in tributary valleys of the Lea may have triggered soil erosion, the accumulation of run-off on the floodplain and the development of peat. The environmental evidence can be used to reconstruct the ancient landscape, providing clues about what people were doing and their impact on the environment. The study of pollen trapped in buried deposits can, for example, reveal forest clearance and cultivation.

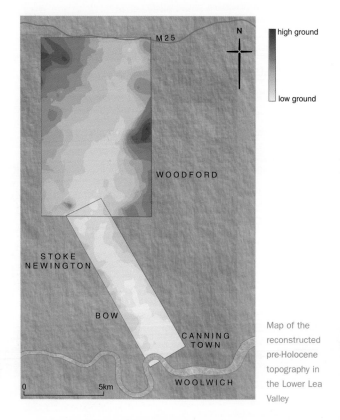

Map of the reconstructed pre-Holocene topography in the Lower Lea Valley

Section showing buried landscape zones in the Bow to Canning Town area

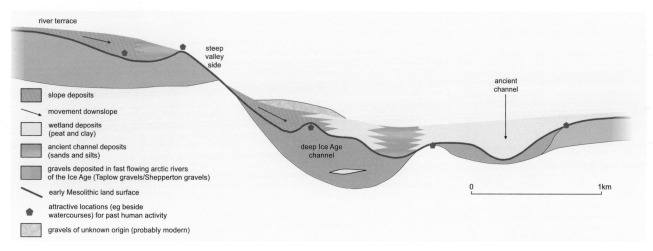

LEFT: Reconstruction view of the Late Bronze Age Lofts Farm settlement near Maldon

The West London landscape

Nicholas Elsden

Archaeological work around Heathrow Airport has revealed both similarities and contrasts between occupation on London's western and eastern gravel landscapes. The majority of Palaeolithic flint tools found in West London, like those from the east, have been washed down the prehistoric Thames and scattered through the terrace gravels. Roving bands of Mesolithic hunter-gatherers left similar evidence of their nomadic lifestyle in both West and East London. Temporary encampments used for butchering reindeer, found beside the River Crane near Uxbridge, can be compared with similar finds from the Lea Valley at Broxbourne.

The Stanwell cursus, a raised ceremonial causeway overlooking the Colne Valley, shows how the surpluses of newly established agricultural communities were used to finance monuments for ceremony and ritual. The circular ritual enclosure at Great Arnold's Field in East London would have served a similar function. But there is no evidence that people in the Heathrow area took up the distinctive pottery of the Beaker culture seen in East London. In the Middle Bronze Age extensive field systems and settlements of round houses enclosed by ditches were established in West London. In East London a similar expansion in the scale of agriculture may not have happened until about 500 years later.

Reconstructing a Middle Bronze Age 'bucket urn' from Cranford Lane, near Heathrow

Earlier Upper Palaeolithic flint blades or flakes from Heathrow Airport, probably dating to between 26,000 and 22,000 BC

There is also less evidence at Heathrow for the Iron Age farmsteads of round houses seen across East London, and nothing to compare to the major fortified settlement of Uphall Camp. But in the Roman period scattered agricultural settlements are found across both West and East London.

Later Neolithic pot in the Mortlake style of Peterborough ware from a West London site (about 3400–2500 BC)

The reconstructed 'bucket urn' of about 1500–1000 BC; the function of the holes is unknown

Prehistoric occupation in the City of London – fact or fiction?

Nick Holder

The first attempt to describe the prehistory of London was written by Geoffrey of Monmouth nearly 900 years ago. His florid account of a London founded by Brutus, newly returned from the victorious Trojan war, has been shown to be fiction. Historians and archaeologists have viewed the City as something of a prehistoric no-man's land, but recent research suggests that central London may be older than we thought. At least two or three farmsteads lay on fertile land east and west of the Walbrook Valley in the Late Bronze Age. It has been suggested that the name Londinium relates to a pre-Celtic name, possibly *Plowonida*, translated as 'boat river' or 'flooding river', describing the tidal lower Thames. The late Bronze Age farmsteads in the City were situated near the point where the tidal *Plowonida* met the upper river, known as *Tamesa*. The Romans may have determined the position of modern London, but the origins of the name itself may be a thousand years older.

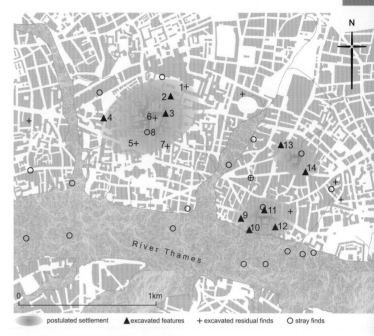

The three late Bronze Age farmsteads of Plowonida, showing their location in relation to the modern City of London

Artist's impression of the Thames with the site of the City of London to the right and the islands and creeks of what later became Southwark to the lower left; compare with the view of the Roman town on p 16

15th-century woodcut illustrating a version of Geoffrey of Monmouth's 12th-century account of the foundation of London by Brutus and the Trojans

Climate change: shaping the landscape

Jane Corcoran

From about half a million years ago (the Quaternary period) the climate has lurched from arctic conditions – known as 'glacials' – to periods when the temperature was as warm as or warmer than today – 'interglacials'. These climatic oscillations have led to continual reshaping of the landscape. Palaeolithic people inhabited Britain from about 650,000 years ago, just before the first major glaciation. Deposits at the interface of the Mucking and Corbets Tey Gravels in the Ilford area provide vital evidence of past environments. The bones of at least 100 mammoths (including the skull of the 'Ilford mammoth', the largest from Britain), many rhinoceri, straight-tusked elephant, lion, brown bear and the giant deer *megaloceros* were collected during 19th-century brickearth digging at quarries such as Uphall Pit, which are now filled in and built over.

Rapid climatic oscillations 10–13,000 years ago marked the transition to the present interglacial stage (the Holocene) and the Mesolithic period. Dramatic changes in climate and vegetation may have taken place within individual lifetimes, and new plants, animal species and people arrived in Britain. The open grassland was quickly colonised by trees, and dense woodland soon cloaked the East London landscape.

The warm, wet climate at the end of the Mesolithic period 6–7000 years ago is sometimes referred to as the climatic optimum. The decline of elm, in around 3500 BC, may have been aggravated or exploited by Neolithic people, for it is in this period that the first evidence for cultivated cereal grain appears alongside an increase in grass and herb species, suggesting the woodland was thinning.

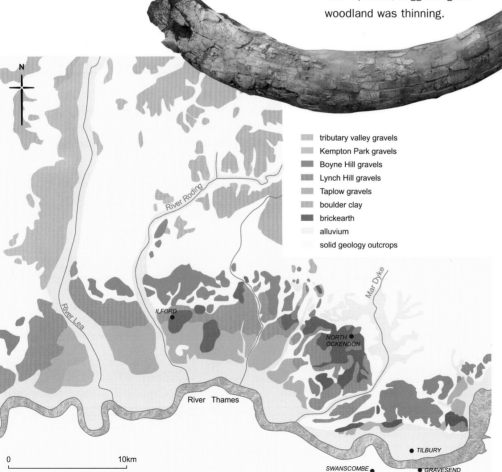

Mammoth's tusk
from London

tributary valley gravels
Kempton Park gravels
Boyne Hill gravels
Lynch Hill gravels
Taplow gravels
boulder clay
brickearth
alluvium
solid geology outcrops

Simplified surface geology illustrating the location of terraces, bedrock exposures, alluvium and boulder clay along the north bank of the Thames in East London

River Roding

River Lea

Mar Dyke

ILFORD

NORTH OCKENDON

River Thames

TILBURY

SWANSCOMBE

GRAVESEND

0   10km

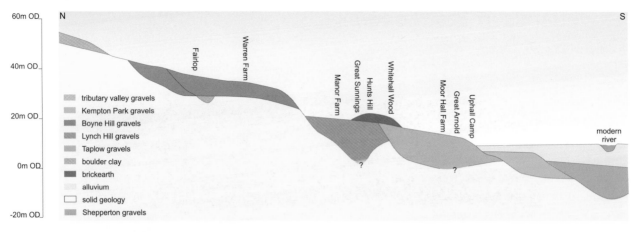

Schematic cross section showing the positions of the East London gravels sites in relation to the landscape north of the Thames

Pollen analysis can provide important information on past climate

Environmental evidence becomes difficult to decipher in the historic period, as the landscape was increasingly managed by humans. Pollen diagrams record the expansion of grasses and weeds of cultivation, a decline in woodland and the introduction of exotic species. Climate has continued to fluctuate over the past 2000 years. Warming took place between AD 700–1300. Average summer and winter temperatures in south-east England in the 12th–13th centuries may have been over a degree higher than today, allowing the expansion of vine growing. Britain then experienced the 'Little Ice Age' of the 14th–18th centuries, with colder, wetter summers and winters, average temperatures 1–3° colder than today and frequent storms. Settlement abandonment, crop failure and floods were a result of the harsher climate of the late medieval and post-medieval periods.

Climatic deterioration from about 2000 BC has been recorded across north-west Europe and the loss of lime trees from the prehistoric forest may have been hastened by Bronze Age farming and increased waterlogging. A decisive shift to cooler, wetter conditions in the Iron Age has been identified through the study of peat bogs. Pollen and sediment data suggest that the mineral-rich soils had become depleted due to the combined impact of human activity and a deteriorating climate. Occupation on the East London gravels would also have been influenced by changes to the floodplains of the Thames, the Lea and the Roding. As sea levels rose, the valley floors became more marshy and estuarine, and dry woodland became wet.

A 1677 painting of people skating on the frozen Thames during the 'Little Ice Age'

The wetlands of East London

Jane Corcoran and Nick Holder

Thanks to centuries of river improvements, the banks of the Thames are now well defined, static and dry. In prehistory the Thames meandered through a floodplain up to 4km wide, with tributary streams and channels changing with the seasons and the marshy woods subject to repeated flooding. Riverside areas in East London were low-lying and became marshlands in later prehistory.

A complex inter-relationship existed between the gravel terraces, the floodplain and the river itself. The Bronze Age inhabitants created a network of tracks and paths – East London's earliest road system – which led through the marshy woodland and connected the Thames to the higher and drier land to the north. Prehistoric people used the contrasting environments of the Thames floodplain for cattle rearing, woodland resources and cultivation. Trackways, made of alder brushwood laid over timber piles driven into the soft wet ground, have been found in Beckton, Rainham and elsewhere in East London. The tracks were usually 1–2m wide, allowing them to be used as droveways for the movement of cattle. Natural clearings or 'islands', surrounded by marshy and wooded fen in the Bronze Age, were used during fishing expeditions or cattle-driving trips.

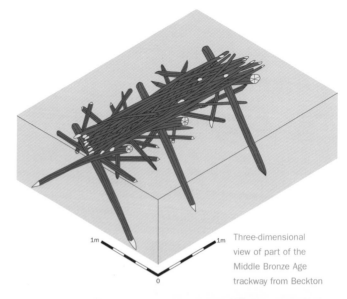

Three-dimensional view of part of the Middle Bronze Age trackway from Beckton

Model of a reconstructed Bronze Age trackway leading through the Thames 'fenland'

Rainham Marshes today provide us with an impression of what East London's wetlands may have looked like

Woodcraft

Dominic Perring

London could not have survived without its woods. Today local forests such as Thames Chase are important for leisure – places for walking and riding which also produce some woodland products. While medieval forests like Epping were protected as places for that most aristocratic of leisure pursuits, hunting, the primary role of the ancient forest was to provide fuel and building materials.

The study of ancient timber structures provides information on forest management and woodworking technology. A surviving timber can tell us about the log and the tree it came from, revealing that both wild and managed woodlands were exploited by Roman London. Some timbers were split from huge, slow-growing oaks that had lived in high, dark wildwood. Others came from small, fast-growing oaks 20–40 years old, coppiced from managed woods.

Studies of the timbers used in the wooden trackways that cross the estuary floodplains of East London show that

A dramatic old oak standing alone in fields at Hunts Hill Farm, where gravel extraction took place around it; the tree has since starred as Charles I's oak in Simon Schama's *History of Britain* and is now an important habitat for rare spiders

coppicing goes back at least to Neolithic times. Coppiced trees are cut close to the ground every few years, letting new wood sprout from the stumps. It is a highly sustainable system, unlike the harvesting of wildwood. By the end of the Roman period, building timbers were mostly taken from younger trees as the number of old-growth trees declined. The farming communities on the gravel terraces of East London exploited managed woodland as well as more distant wildwood. Some forests remained in public ownership – especially sacred woods. It seems that farming communities around London kept something of their pre-Roman 'rustic' character, at least in carpentry techniques, as timbers were often shaped by a woodman's axe rather than sawn, as was standard practice in Roman London.

During the Roman period, the woods around London were dominated by oak. There was also a small amount of alder, but elm and beech, though present, were almost never used. An elm branch found in a well at Hunts Hill Farm is the only piece of Roman elm known from the region, and its scarcity may indicate an outbreak of elm disease.

Late Saxon and early medieval timber structures in London made abundant use of trees that had started growing in the early 5th century, suggesting that woodlands had regrown after the Roman period. But by 1250 much of this woodland had been felled and local wildwood timber disappeared from use. Without this habitat, bears, wolves, wild swine and wild cattle also disappeared. By the 14th century, oak boards were being imported from Europe. The British tradition of large-scale, unsustainable harvesting of foreign wildwoods had begun.

Coppiced trees at Thames Chase Community Forest

Cattle ranching on the borders of London

Dominic Perring with Kevin Rielly

Although sheep farming may have been more important to the prehistoric rural economy, cattle also had an important role – wherever grain was grown it also made sense to keep cattle to pull the plough. Over time, dairying and beef farming grew as London's demand for surplus production increased.

Late Bronze Age and Iron Age cattle droveways have been identified at Hunts Hill Farm and other East London sites such as Gun Hill, near Tilbury, where the management of livestock is revealed by droveways linking pasture and stock enclosures. Iron Age cattle were a Celtic shorthorn variety and cattle herds were a means of representing wealth. Cattle were mainly kept for traction and dairying, although the study of bones shows that younger cattle were also culled, suggesting that they were being raised for beef.

Celtic shorthorn cattle

At the time of the conquest, the Roman army imported much of its food, and corn initially came from the eastern Mediterranean. But Britain was normally self-sufficient in grain and, according to late Roman historians, was able to export grain to support military campaigns elsewhere.

During the course of the 2nd and 3rd centuries AD some farmers had invested in stock improvement, and larger cattle were introduced. This was also a period of

Cattle shoulder blade – possible remains of a cured beef shoulder joint

investment in new field systems and paddocks, as the countryside was more intensively farmed in order to generate higher taxes, many of which were collected in kind. The cattle produced on Essex estates were probably destined for urban markets, with butchery taking place at roadside settlements *en route* to Londinium. Large amounts of butchered cattle bone have been found at Old Ford and Shadwell, east of the city. Other cattle may have been driven into the urban centre or fattened nearby. Cattle by-products such as leather were important to the urban economy, and tanning pits were commonplace.

Leather goods from London; the sole of a Roman shoe

Cattle remained a large part of the economy of medieval and later East London, with tanning works in Barking and West Ham. The southern part of the parish of Dagenham was marshland pasture used for sheep grazing in the 17th and early 18th centuries. Although attempts were made to reclaim the land, it was too expensive to plough and at risk of flooding. Daniel Defoe observed 'that the great part of these levels, especially those on the side of East Tilbury, are held by the farmers, cow-keepers, and grasing butchers who live in and near London, and that they are generally stocked (all the winter-half year) with large fat sheep'. Cattle and sheep are still kept on the Rainham marshes today.

Some of the old gravel workings at Belhus Woods have been allowed to regenerate naturally without landscaping

Trade and exchange

Dominic Perring

Archaeological findings provide important insights into past economies as the goods and belongings found on excavation sites provide us with a chronology of events and evidence of trade. There was already trade and contact with the near Continent in the Bronze Age. Pottery survives well in the ground and in many cases can be traced to a particular source. Some pottery can be related to trade in particular commodities, such as Roman amphorae, which contained wine and oil. Other pots can be associated with social practices and cultural affiliations.

Trade was not the only way in which goods were moved. Early Roman London was a focus for the movement of military supplies and personnel. Late Roman and medieval estates sought self-sufficiency by collecting produce from a variety of landholdings in different parts of the country. Taxes, especially when raised in kind, encouraged the movement of goods, as did the exchange of gifts by the politically powerful. These networks gave towns and roadside settlements access to a wider range of imported goods than the smaller rural settlements of the East London terraces. But Roman pottery was made and moved in such large quantities that even the more remote rural sites had Roman storage vessels and tablewares.

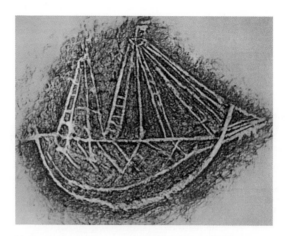

Medieval ship graffito on wall in Rainham parish church

In medieval times, Barking was the home of a fishing fleet and Rainham exported wool to France, whilst London was the hub of the grain trade. Long before this, farming produced surpluses needed to feed a growing population and pay rising taxes in the Late Iron Age and Roman period. The importance of creating a surplus can be traced back to prehistoric times, when cultivation was expanded into marginal lands and forests and there was a shift from sheep to arable farming.

Coinage is usually seen as evidence for the operation of market exchange, but prehistoric East London saw the circulation of mainly high value gold and silver coins, such as the potins from Uphall Camp. This coinage is more likely to have been a token of exchange between kings and lords than a useful medium for ordinary trade. British potins were probably made in north Kent from the late 2nd to late 1st century BC. They were the first British coins, perhaps modelled on similar central Gaulish coins, and were closely associated with a network of major sites spanning the Thames estuary.

Roman amphorae

Late 7th-century silver *sceattas* from Mucking

Industry and production

Dominic Perring

Before the modern era, small-scale industrial activity was scattered across the countryside, and was not centralised and commercialised. The most common activities were processing local wool and weaving textiles. Bronze Age loom weights and spindle whorls, used in spinning and weaving, show the importance of cloth production. Large numbers of triangular fired clay weights found at East London sites are thought to be from the Late Iron Age. The weights were probably used to tension the warp threads on an upright loom, although weights from Moor Hall Farm may be too heavy for the task.

Bronze Age loom weights

A large group of Saxon loom weights visible on a hut floor at Mucking

Excavating 'Belgic bricks' and triangular weights, found along with some iron objects and a little pot and bone at Moor Hall Farm, perhaps a ritual deposit

Metalworking has often been connected with a magical alchemy and it is not unusual to find industry near religious and elite sites, but traces of industrial activity were also found on ordinary sites including those on the East London gravels. Iron Age metalworking debris and associated tools were found at Uphall Camp and Hunts Hill Farm, providing important evidence for the development of technology and local craft activity. Copper waste from Hunts Hill may have come from a bronze smith's workshop.

Roman pottery manufacture was widespread throughout the region. A late Roman pottery kiln may have operated at Hunts Hill and other kilns have been excavated at Shoebury, Rawreth, Mucking and Orsett. These kilns produced functional items such as storage vessels, which may have been manufactured in association with food processing.

Salt extraction along the Lower Thames Estuary surged in the early Roman period, and meant that local produce could be preserved and packed for export. Coastal 'red hills' – distinctive mounds of debris, fire-reddened soil and broken coarse pottery known as 'briquetage' – are associated with the salt industry.

Post-medieval agricultural and commercial industrialisation took place on a much larger scale. Some evidence of the trend was found at the East London excavations. Industrialisation was the dominating theme of the last 100 years. Today factories and container depots stretch from Dagenham to Rainham.

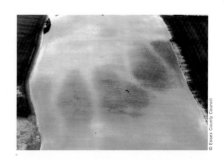

Air photograph showing ploughed 'red hills' associated with Roman salt making, in south Essex

Ritual and ceremony in the prehistoric landscape

Richard Bradley

One of the problems of studying Britain's prehistoric landscape is the disparity between the evidence of every-day life and what is often described as 'ritual' activity. Our perceptions of the past may be distorted by the survival of such impressive monuments as Avebury and Stonehenge. There is another problem, too. The clearest indications of ritual and ceremony come from earlier prehistory: the periods between about 4000 and 1500 BC that are described by archaeologists as the Neolithic and the Early Bronze Age.

In common with many regions with access to the North Sea, East London presents an unusual picture. Major earthwork monuments are rare, and stone structures are altogether absent. There are few monumental burial mounds, and specialised enclosures (like the Orsett causewayed enclosure) are uncommon and small after about 3000 BC. The evidence for ritual and the celebration of the dead comes from less imposing structures. As well as the 'long barrows' that typify the Wessex downland, there was an early tradition of building circular burial mounds, circular earthwork enclosures known as henges (such as the ring ditch at Great Arnold's Field), and wooden structures like 'Seahenge' in Norfolk. These places may be more typical of development in prehistoric England than the better-known archaeological sites that still survive above ground.

Artist's impression of Neolithic ritual activity at the Springfield cursus, near Chelmsford

Building a Bronze Age barrow

It is all too easy to suppose that public and ritual ceremony took place in special areas, well away from the settlements in which people lived. That may not be true; the kinds of artefacts deposited in 'ritual' structures are the same as those found at ordinary habitation sites. The crucial difference concerns the formality with which artefacts had been used and deposited. The same generally applies to earlier prehistoric material, including human remains, deposited in rivers like the Thames.

From about 1500 BC there are more surviving traces of settlement. The landscape was sometimes divided up by a network of field and boundary ditches, and burial mounds (as at Fairlop Quarry) became smaller before disappearing altogether. We could assume that ritual and ceremonial had lost their power over the people living on the East London gravels, but this would be wrong. Burials can often be found in small cremation cemeteries located near to the fields and houses (as at Great Sunnings Farm), and the remains of human cremations were scattered across the settled area. Specialised, perhaps ceremonial, deposits of animal remains, pottery (as in the well at Moor Hall Farm) and metalwork have been found alongside the houses, fields, grain storage pits and ponds that provided the framework for daily life. More elaborate artefacts, in particular weapons, were deliberately deposited in watery locations. The River Thames contains one of the largest collections of prehistoric metalwork in Europe, some of it associated with human bones.

Ritual still played a central part in people's lives, but over the 1500 years before the Roman conquest had become more closely integrated into the workings of everyday life.

Pit with remains of an Early Iron Age pot at Great Sunnings Farm; possibly part of a ritual deposit

Managing the Thames

Pamela Greenwood and Peter Rowsome

The Thames has served both as a route – linking London to the sea – and a frontier, separating Kent from Essex. Ferries and bridges have been maintained for centuries, even when the opposing banks were held by different tribes. There is evidence for a ferry at Rainham possibly from the pre-Roman period to the 19th century. The earliest known bridge was built in the Bronze Age, near the upper reach of the tide at Vauxhall. The first true bridge across the Thames was built by the Romans in about AD 50, near present-day London Bridge. Over 1800 years would elapse before a bridge was established further downriver – Tower Bridge, completed in 1894. Several tunnels now pass beneath the river and the world's second longest cable-stayed bridge connects Dartford and Thurrock. Plans are afoot for a new crossing – the Thames Gateway Bridge – linking Beckton to Thamesmead.

Most people think of the estuary of the Thames as lying far downstream of central London, but technically it now starts 14 miles upstream of London at Teddington Lock. Over the millennia the extent of the estuary has varied dramatically according to the vagaries of sea level and tide.

Vauxhall Bronze Age bridge leading to an island in the Thames

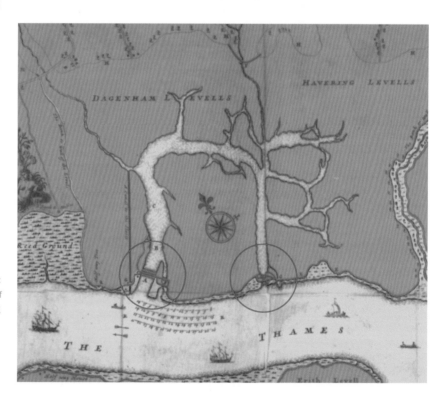

Flooding on the Thames: the Dagenham Breach of 1707 (left) and Havering Gulf of 1591 (right)

The proposed Thames Gateway Bridge will link Beckton and Thamesmead; it is expected to cost £450 million and be completed by 2013

The Thames Barrier at Woolwich now protects riverside residents from flooding, at least temporarily. People have struggled since medieval times to keep the river at bay with walls, ditches and dykes. Today sea walls are being experimentally breached in line with new theories that marshes are the best way to absorb the force of floodwater, as they used to.

By the 19th century the Thames was notorious as a dirty river and the source of disease and infection. Malaria – known as the ague by medieval doctors – was endemic in Rainham, the marshes being ideal for mosquitoes. Raw sewage and slaughterhouse waste made the river extremely unpleasant as far downstream as Barking, until Bazalgette built the first proper sewers in the 1860s, after the 'Great Stink' of 1858 forced Parliament to act.

Although essential for trade and prosperity, the river has also made London, Kent and Essex vulnerable to invasion. The Roman forts along the 'Saxon shore' included Bradwell to the north and Reculver to the south of the river mouth. Sea-borne Germanic immigrants in the 5th and 6th century made their way inland up the Thames and its tributaries. Vikings attacked London in the 9th century, bringing their ships up the Thames, as did the Dutch in the 17th century. Forts have been built along the lower reaches of the river since the Iron Age. Henry VIII constructed Tilbury Fort, and later defences include Palmerston's Coalhouse Fort at East Tilbury and the coastal defences from World War I and II.

The dirty Thames: Tenniel cartoon of 1858, showing the 'silent highwayman'

Connections to the sea were important to East London; here we can see Barking town quay in the early 20th century

Defending the Thames: Tilbury Fort as it would have appeared in the mid 19th century; the fort was garrisoned up to the 1920s but it was never put to the test

Farming on the East London gravels

John Giorgi

Evidence for prehistoric and Roman farming on the East London gravels survives as charred plant remains and animal bone. Plant remains, mainly cereal grains accidentally burnt during processing and cooking, were found at Uphall Camp and several other sites.

Wheat and six-row hulled barley were the main cereals that were cultivated and used in the area. The wheat grains were mainly emmer and spelt, two primitive glume wheats, but there was some evidence for free-threshing bread wheat, which is still grown and used today. Chaff fragments (husks of the grains) and arable weed seeds such as stinking mayweed, a problem for farmers, provide evidence of harvesting and processing.

Wheat was probably used exclusively for human food; the husked wheats, emmer and spelt, would have been suitable for unleavened loaves. The Romans made a number of different breads, including *artophites*, light leavened bread made from the best wheat flour. Cereal grains may have also been used for making porridge or gruel, or added as whole grains to stews (pottage) or soups. The Romans made gruel from barley or spelt wheat known as *puls* or *pulmentus*, similar to Italian polenta. Flax seeds were also added to these soups, the oil content enriching the food.

Prehistoric ploughing along the Thames

Other wild foods, whose fruits and seeds were found, would have been gathered from hedgerows and woods. Waterlogged deposits from wells and pits at Hunts Hill Farm included seeds of blackberries/raspberries, elderberries and sloe/blackthorn as well as hazelnut shell fragments. Wild fruits would have provided an important seasonal food, while the hazelnuts could have been stored for winter use and the various berries made into preserves or included in alcoholic drinks.

Common vegetables such as peas, horse-beans, onions and green leaf crops would have also been an important part of the diet, but these remains have not survived on the East London sites.

Emmer wheat

Barley was used for food and producing malt for beer, a practice that may date back to the end of the Neolithic period. Cauldron-like vessels found at several of the sites may have been used for producing beer and are dated to the Iron Age. Barley was also used as animal fodder, particularly for horses during the Roman period.

A reconstructed Iron Age oven at Butser Ancient Farm, Hampshire

Market gardening for London

Pamela Greenwood

Towards the end of the 18th century farmers in south-west Essex began to grow vegetables for the London market. Peas and beans were 'first gathered green' – not mature as for dried pulses – in Dagenham parish in about 1788. Disputes raged here from 1811–40 about the rate of tithes for peas, beans, coleseed and potatoes. Potatoes, first grown around 1800, were very important to the local economy, whilst watercress was grown along the River Roding at Uphall. In the 15th–17th centuries vineyards were established around Barking.

Market gardening increased during the 19th century and by the 1890s several farmers had begun to grow fruit, including one farm in Dagenham operated by Wilkin & Sons of Tiptree. This was so profitable that new farmers flocked to the area from as far away as Devon and Scotland. Around Marks Gate, wheat, barley and oats were grown alongside fruit and vegetables. Rainham was famous for cauliflowers and even had a pub named after them. Night soil, sewage and slaughterhouse waste was used to fertilize the fields, making for a very unpleasant smelling area.

London vegetable markets depended on deliveries made by horse-drawn carts. At the end of the 19th century carts left Dagenham in the evening and reached Covent Garden in the early hours. On the way back they picked up manure at Whitechapel and finally arrived home after a 24-hour round-trip. The horses knew the route and if the drivers were found asleep at the market, the cart would be turned around and the horse would obediently go home with a full load.

A farm cart loaded with cabbages in Upminster parish

Market gardening and farming declined as the area became increasingly built-up, but some agricultural production has continued. When gravel extraction started at Warren Farm in 1988, the Fowlers were still growing cereals, potatoes and oilseed rape. Their 'Bonzer Potatoes' are still sold at the farm shop and at the roadside.

Watercress beds on the banks of the River Roding, about 1895

Bean pickers pose for a photograph at Hacton Farm in Upminster parish

The growth of settlement

Pamela Greenwood

Over the last 400,000 years or so human settlement of East London has changed dramatically. In milder interludes between glaciations, early Palaeolithic hunting groups lived in the open by streams and riverbanks, probably in makeshift huts or tents, but in the colder periods they needed substantial clothing, shelter and fires. After the end of the Ice Age nomadic hunting families lived in temporary camps, first in the tundra and then in the new woodlands.

We have better evidence for houses, both round and rectangular, from Neolithic Britain. Isolated farmsteads or groups of houses and small fields were established in clearings in the woods. Bronze Age farmers cleared more of the woodland, and lived in post-built round houses, sometimes in small enclosures as at Hunts Hill Farm. 'Ring forts' constructed in prominent places may have been higher status farmsteads set among larger fields, while others were ceremonial.

Artist's impression of an Iron Age settlement at Tongham, Surrey

Reconstructed Iron Age round house at Butser Ancient Farm, Hampshire

Reconstruction of Middle Bronze Age houses and fields at Ardleigh, near Colchester

For much of the Iron Age the people of the Thames estuary lived in round houses in small farmsteads or even villages, although Uphall Camp was a rare example of a large tribal centre. Towards the end of the Iron Age people began to build rectangular or roughly square houses, and fields have been found at Hunts Hill Farm and Aveley. Some rectangular enclosures on higher ground, such as Moor Hall Farm and Orsett Cock, may have been religious centres. The increased evidence of settlement suggests that the population was increasing.

Many of the small farming settlements continued into the Roman period but there were also additions to the landscape – including extensive field systems and grander buildings. Big estates and distant owners, as well as the influence of Londinium, would have changed the appearance of the countryside.

In the early part of the Saxon period both small and large settlements were established, with cemeteries nearby. Later on, people began to gather together around the church and manor house, giving rise to villages like Rainham and Dagenham.

Reconstruction drawing of an Early Saxon settlement at Hurst Park, Surrey

From the later medieval period onwards settlement was a familiar mixture of farms, villages, and small towns. There were a few manors, some moated, and the mansions of the rich. Maps show the increasing pace of settlement, the rise of market gardening and the growth of industry. Roads, railways and housing all expanded again after World War I.

The parish church of St Helen and St Giles, Rainham, dates from the Norman period

A reconstruction of the royal palace at Havering as it may have appeared in 1578

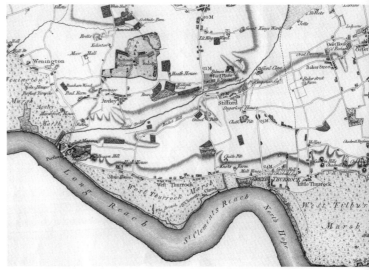

Part of Chapman and André's 1777 map showing some of the earliest quarries in south Essex

A sea of terraced housing forms a typical East London view of what was once farmland and forest

Rainham village in about 1910

Quarrying and restoring the landscape

Pamela Greenwood

People have used gravel and stone for thousands of years, since they first made handaxes and other tools from local flint taken from the Thames terraces, and dug as nodules from the chalk outcrops around Purfleet. Small-scale digging for gravel later provided material for floors and enabled the improvement of paths and roads, such as the Roman road at Warren Farm. The Roman building at Warren Farm was built from fresh flint nodules mined in a chalk-bearing area such as Purfleet.

The earliest recorded gravel pits are in the Dagenham Corridor, with extraction tending to move eastwards over time. Much of the area around Old Church, Romford, was dug away in the 1800s, but it was not until the 20th century that centralised records of quarrying were made by the then Greater London Council and local authorities. Today the London Borough of Havering is compiling the first definitive map of mineral working in order to record contamination, landfill and related environmental problems.

Larger-scale gravel extraction began with the rise of road building in the 18th century, but for a long time quarries were hand-dug. After World War II both the rate of and the areas taken up for gravel extraction increased. By the late 1970s mineral companies were extracting deposits that they had ignored in the 1950s and 1960s, in order to supply the increase in house building and big road construction schemes, such as the M25. Draglines, box scrapers and larger trucks allowed huge areas to be quarried in just a few years. This meant that archaeologists were faced with the challenge of investigating hundreds of hectares at sites such as Mucking.

Processing plants at Baldwins Farm, south of Upminster, are used to sieve and separate the aggregates into different grades down to fine sand

Courtesy of T Bovis

An excavator waits atop a heap of gravel which is about to be hauled away for processing

The destination of much of London's rubbish remains landfill sites – many of them in East London

By the 1970s much of the gravel terrace in South Havering and around Thurrock was a wasteland. Quarries that had been worked out were left open or became ugly tips and landfill sites for London's rubbish, with methane fires and hazardous waste adding to the problem. Badly restored land unsuitable for agriculture became derelict or rough grazing for ponies and cattle. A few companies took an early lead in restoring the land, such as St Albans Sand and Gravel. Other sites have been reinstated as small reservoirs or lakes for leisure and wildlife use. The creation of Thames Chase Community Forest is allowing more land to be restored and hedgerows and trees planted, creating new woodland.

The regenerated Hunts Hill Farm quarries form an ideal wildlife refuge

Natural regeneration of the gravel pits at Whitehall Wood has created lakes, providing leisure amenities and wildlife habitat

Places to visit

Belhus Woods country park
Romford Road, Aveley, South Ockendon RM15 4XJ
Tel: 01708 865628

Butser Ancient Farm
Chalton near Petersfield, Hampshire
Tel: 02392 598838
www.butser.org.uk

Coalhouse Fort
East Tilbury
Tel: 01375 844 203
www.coalhousefort.co.uk

Museum in Docklands
No. 1 Warehouse, West India Quay, Hertsmere Road, London E14 4AL
Tel: 0870 444 3856   Email: info@museumindocklands.org.uk
www.museumindocklands.org.uk

Museum of London: 'London before London' gallery
London Wall, London EC2Y 5HN
Tel: 0870 444 3852 (national call rates in UK) +44 (0)20 7600 3699
www.museumoflondon.org.uk

Rainham Marshes nature reserve
New Tank Hill Road, Purfleet
Tel: 01705 520145
www.rainhammarshes.org.uk

Redbridge Museum
Central Library, Clements Road, Ilford IG1 1EA
Tel: 020 8708 2432

Tilbury fort
Located $^1/_2$ mile E of Tilbury off A126
Tel: 01375 858489
www.english-heritage.org.uk

Thames Barrier Park
The Pavilion, Barrier Point Road, London E16 2HP
Tel: 020 7511 4111
www.thamesbarrierpark.org.uk

Thames Chase Community Forest
The Forest Centre, Broadfields, Pike Lane, Cranham
Upminster RM14 3NS
Tel: 01708 641880   Email: enquiries@thameschase.org.uk
www.thameschase.org.uk

Thurrock Museum
Thameside Complex, Orsett Road, Grays RM17 5DX
Tel: 01375 385484   Email: thurrock.museum@thurrock.gov.uk
www.thurrock.gov.uk/museum

Valence House Museum
Becontree Avenue, Dagenham RM8 3HT
Tel: 020 8270 6865
www.barking-dagenham.gov.uk/4-valence

Websites

ALSF Projects Online: www.english-heritage.org.uk/admisremote/ALSFOnline

English Heritage: www.english-heritage.org.uk

Museum of London Archaeology Service: www.molas.org.uk

Archaeology and history of South Essex: www.finestprospect.org.uk

Essex Archives Online: www.seax.essexcc.gov.uk

Further reading

P Ackroyd, 2000 *London: the biography*, London

N Brown, 2000 *Splendid and permanent pageants: archaeological and historical reconstruction pictures of Essex*, Chelmsford

N Brown, 2005 *Finest prospect: the archaeology of south Essex*, Chelmsford

H Clout (ed), 1991 *The Times London history atlas*, London

J Cotton and N Merriman, in prep, *London before history: prehistory in the middle and lower Thames Valley*

S Curtis, 2000 *Dagenham and Rainham past*, Chichester

B Evans, 1992 *Bygone Dagenham and Rainham*, Chichester

S Halliday, 1999 *The great stink of London: Sir Joseph Bazalgette and the cleansing of the Victorian capital*, Stroud

I Haynes, H Sheldon and L Hannigan, 2000 *London under ground: the archaeology of a city*, Oxford

J Kemp, 2001 *Prehistoric and Roman Essex*, Stroud

MoLAS, 2000 *The archaeology of Greater London: an assessment of archaeological evidence for human presence in the area now covered by Greater London*, London

N Merriman, 1990 *Prehistoric London*, London

M Pitts and M Roberts, 1997 *Fairweather Eden: life in Britain half a million years ago as revealed by the excavations at Boxgrove*, London

C Thomas, 2003 *London's archaeological secrets: a world city revealed*, New Haven and London

B Watson, 2004 *Old London Bridge lost and found*, London

G Weightman and S Humphries, 1983 *The making of modern London 1815–1914*, London

B Weinreb and C Hibbert, 1983 *The London encyclopaedia*, London

P Ziegler, 1995 *London at war, 1939–1945*, New York